Lenten Bible Study Series C

Study Guide

William Ney
Donald Schiemann

SAINT LOUIS

Edited by Thomas J. Doyle

This publication is available in braille and in large print for the visually impaired. Write to the Library for the Blind, 1333 S. Kirkwood Rd., St. Louis, MO 63122-7295; or call 1-800-433-3954.

Copyright © 2000 Concordia Publishing House
3558 S. Jefferson Avenue, St. Louis, MO 63118-3968
Manufactured in the United States of America

1 2 3 4 5 6 7 8 9 10   09 08 07 06 05 04 03 02 01 00

Contents

About the Series

This course is one of six Advent-Lent adult Bible study courses. The Bible studies in the series are tied to the three-year lectionary. These studies give participants the opportunity to explore the Old Testament lesson, the Epistle lesson, and the Gospel lesson appointed for each Sunday during Advent and Lent.

Each course will draw you deeper into those parts of Scripture that deal with some of the greatest events in the life of Jesus—His incarnation and His passion. Although these courses may be used any time of year, they were originally designed for the two most reflective seasons of the church year—Advent and Lent.

Each study is designed to help participants draw conclusions about each of the lessons appointed for a Sunday, compare and contrast the lessons, discover a unifying theme (if possible), and apply the theme to their lives. The Leaders Guide for each course provides additional textual information on appointed lessons, answers to the questions in the Study Guide, a suggested process for teaching the study, and devotional or worship activities tied to the theme.

May the Holy Spirit richly bless you as you study God's Word.

The First Sunday in Lent

(Deuteronomy 26:5–10; Romans 10:8b–13; Luke 4:1–13)

Focus

Theme: Been There, Done That

Law/Gospel Focus

By nature we are spiritually homeless people. Our sin has created an insurmountable barrier between us and God. Nothing we can do can prevent our final death in the wilderness of sin and despair. God, however, left His heavenly throne to rescue us. By His victory over sin, death, and Satan, He offers heavenly hope and a home to all. He promises, "Everyone who calls on the name of the Lord will be saved" (Romans 10:3).

Objectives

As God works in our heart and mind through His Word, the Holy Spirit will enable us to see that
1. God's grace is sufficient for the worst of sinners;
2. God knows the challenges and temptations we face;
3. God has defeated the power of sin, death, and Satan;
4. through faith in Christ we are heirs to a new life;
5. our new life in Christ includes the promise of eternal life in heaven.

Opening Worship

Speak responsively the following prayer:

Leader: O Lord God Most High, almighty Fortress and Protector, we praise You for Your providence which has brought us to this hour.

Participants: In the midst of many dangers and temptations, we are still Your children by Your grace through faith in Jesus Christ.

Leader: Trusting in Your grace and mercy and believing Your promises to hear our prayers, we come before You with praise and thanksgiving.

Participants: We give You special thanks, O Lord, for sending Your Son into the world to become true man.

Leader: Thank You that when He was tempted, as we are, He did not yield to sin but remained obedient to You for our sake.

Participants: When Satan tempts us through our fleshly appetites, the riches of this world, and our love for honor and prestige, help us to use Your Word as our weapon against him.

Leader: For inspiring men to write it, translate it, and print it so that it is readily available to us, we give You hearty thanks.

(Theodore P. Bornhoeft, *Prayers Responsively* [CPH: 1984], p. 158)

Introduction

Homeless people—they are in all our cities and towns. We have all seen them at one time or another. They live in cardboard boxes. They eat food scraps. From time to time, they approach us for "spare change." In cold winters, some of them freeze to death.

It's interesting to see how people react to the homeless. Some look at them with pity. Others are repulsed by them. Most ignore them. Can you imagine the reaction of most people if someone were to suggest that they take a homeless person into their home or that they trade places with a homeless person?

That's exactly what Jesus did. He came into a world of people who were spiritually lost, dying, and homeless. He could see plainly the hideous, repulsive, sinful condition of people. It is truly a measure of God's grace that He came into this world as one of us. He actually took our place so that we could live in His heavenly home. He left His home so that we would have an eternal home. Truly, our Savior has "been there and done that" for us.

1. What experiences have you had with homeless people? What parallels can we draw between being physically homeless and spiritually homeless?

2. From God's perspective, our spiritual state of homelessness was far more repulsive than any physical homeless condition could be. What moved God to have His Son take our place? Read John 3:16.

3. A "substitute" takes our place. Jesus took our place under the Law and suffered what we should have suffered because of our sins. What are the blessings bestowed on us because of this heavenly substitution?

Inform

Read Deuteronomy 26:5–10; Romans 10:8b–13; and Luke 4:1–13. Then read the following summaries of the lessons appointed for the First Sunday in Lent.

Deuteronomy 26:5–10—When the Israelites entered the land of Canaan they were to give a special offering to the Lord. An essential part of that offering was a recital of how God delivered them into Canaan. This reminded them that Jacob, the father of their 12 tribal ancestors, was the son of an Aramean mother, that he was married to two Aramean wives, that he lived many years in Paddan Aram, and that he spent his final years in Egypt. In short, he was a "wandering Aramean." The Israelites, Jacob's descendants, suffered under the yoke of Egyptian slavery. These people without an earthly home or hope were delivered by God in a wonderful and miraculous way and now lived in a land and a home He had given them as part of His covenant promise (Genesis 13:12–17).

Romans 10:8b–13—We proclaim through faith that "Jesus is Lord." We believe with our hearts that He has risen from the dead. This belief is at the center of saving faith, and it is God's absolute promise that whoever believes in Christ's resurrection—whether Jew or Gentile—will be saved.

Luke 4:1–13—After His Baptism, Jesus was led by the Spirit into the desert, where He fasted for 40 days and was tempted by Satan. Three major temptations are recorded here. Jesus resisted all these temptations, and these victories set in motion the direction of His entire ministry. He is victor over sin and Satan by His death on the cross and triumphant resurrection from the dead.

1. In what sense could the Israelites have been considered homeless?

2. Given the background of the Israelites as described in our Old Testament lesson, were they, from a human viewpoint, a likely choice to be God's people?

3. What are the standards by which people tend to judge others? What are the standards by which God judges? Read 1 Samuel 16:7.

4. When God looks into our hearts, what does He seek? Read Romans 10:9.

5. In the world of business and politics, it is said, "It's not *what* you know, it's *who* you know." Do our connections influence God in any way? Read Romans 10:12.

6. The Bible speaks of Jesus as our substitute. The first thing Jesus did after His Baptism was to go into the desert, where He fasted and was tempted. Why was that a necessary part of God's plan for our salvation? Read Hebrews 4:14–16.

7. What did Jesus use to resist Satan's temptations?

Connect

He who is the Bread of Life began His ministry hungering.
He who is the Water of Life ended His ministry thirsting.
Christ hungered as man and fed the hungry as God.
He was weary, and yet He is our rest.
He paid tribute, and yet He is the King.
He was called a devil, and yet He cast out devils.
He prayed, and yet He hears our prayers.
He wept, and yet He dries our tears.
He was sold for 30 pieces of silver, and yet He redeemed the world.

He was led as a lamb to the slaughter and is called the
Good Shepherd.
He died and by dying destroyed death.—Anonymous

1. When we struggle with sin, how is it comforting for you to
know that God has "been there, done that"?

2. In what ways can we be compared to the Israelites as they
are described in the Old Testament lesson? Read John 15:16.

3. Isaiah 52:14 and 53:2–3 describe Jesus as the Suffering
Servant. How is He described in His appearance? How is this a
description of the world for which He is a substitute?

Vision

During This Week

1. As you relate to other people this week, pray that you might
be able to see them as God sees them—as people for whom Christ
died.
2. Pray for those you know who are spiritually homeless, and
look for ways to invite them to God's home.

Closing Worship

Sing or speak together the following stanzas of "My Song Is
Love Unknown" (*LW* 91).

My song is love unknown, my Savior's love to me,
Love to the loveless shown that they might lovely be.
Oh, who am I that for my sake
My Lord should take frail flesh and die?

He came from His blest throne salvation to bestow;
But men made strange, and none the longed-for Christ
would know.
But, oh, my Friend, my Friend indeed,
Who at my need His life did spend!

In life no house, no home my Lord on earth might have;
In death no friendly tomb but what a stranger gave.
What may I say? Heav'n was His home
But mine the tomb wherein He lay.

Here might I stay and sing, no story so divine!
Never was love, dear King, never was grief like Thine,
This is my friend, in whose sweet praise
I all my days could gladly spend!

Scripture Lessons for Next Sunday

In preparation for the Second Sunday in Lent, read Jeremiah
26:8–15; Philippians 3:17–4:1; and Luke 13:31–35.

Session 2

The Second Sunday in Lent

(Jeremiah 26:8–15; Philippians 3:17–4:1; Luke 13:31–35)

Focus

Theme: Don't Shoot the Messenger!

Law/Gospel Focus

People often clothe themselves in a veneer of self-righteousness. They may even have an outward appearance of godliness. Ultimately, however, every human hides a heart and life diseased by sin. God's messengers speak a message that shatters the veneer and exposes the diseased heart. People do not want to hear, and their response is often anger toward the messengers. God promises, however, that His Word will not return empty (Isaiah 55:10–11). Through Christ, the living Word, we find healing for the heart and soul.

Objectives

That by the power of the Holy Spirit at work in our hearts through His Word, we will
1. confess our "comfortable" and our "uncomfortable" sins;
2. find our joy and our crown in Christ our Savior;
3. joyfully and eagerly anticipate Christ as He comes to us now in Word and Sacrament and as He will come again to take us to our heavenly home.

Opening Worship

Sing or speak together "Blessed Be the God of Israel" (*With One Voice* 725). Then pray the prayer that follows:
Bless'd be the God of Israel who comes to set us free
And raises up new hope for us: a Branch from David's tree.

So have the prophets long declared that with a mighty arm
God would turn back our enemies and all who wish us harm.

With promised mercy will God still the covenant recall,
The oath once sworn to Abraham, from foes to save us all;
That we might worship without fear and offer lives of praise,
In holiness and righteousness to serve God all our days.

My child, as prophet of the Lord you will prepare the way,
To tell God's people they are saved from sin's eternal sway.
Then shall God's mercy from on high shine forth and never cease
To drive away the gloom of death and lead us into peace.

O God, whose glory it is always to have mercy, be gracious
to all who have gone astray from Your ways and bring them
again with penitent hearts and steadfast faith to embrace and
hold fast the unchangeable truth of Your Word; through
Jesus Christ, Your Son, our Lord, who lives and reigns with
You and the Holy Spirit, one God, now and forever. Amen.

Introduction

"Abortion is killing."
"Homosexuality is sinful."
"Doctor-assisted suicide is wrong."
"Without saving faith in Christ, people are eternally lost."
Talk about politically incorrect statements! To make such state-
ments publicly would invite accusations of narrow-mindedness,
intolerance, and lovelessness. One might even be considered on
the fringe of extremism.

People don't like to hear that the accepted status quo may be
wrong. The preaching of the Law and the call to repentance is
never warmly received. Such a call, by its very nature, implies
there is something wrong with our lives and something wrong with
us. It's easier to say that the problem is not with us—it's with the
messenger. What right does he have to say such things?

The preaching of the Law and the call to repentance, however, have a very specific purpose. When we realize that the problem is with us and not the messenger, we come to grips with our own sinfulness and our urgent need for a Savior.

1. What is the purpose of the Law? Read Romans 7:7. In light of Romans 7:25, describe the tension that occurs when we hear the Law preached and applied to our lives. Does the Law, at times, make you feel uncomfortable? Why?

2. Self-righteousness is a defense mechanism that we often activate when hearing the Law. We attempt to justify our actions by saying that the Law isn't fair, that our circumstances are special, or that we have compensated by doing more than is necessary in other areas of our lives. Frequently people twist the Law to speak for them rather than against them. Read Mark 7:9–13. How did people use or abuse the Law in Jesus' day?

3. God offers a better solution. Read Philippians 3:8–9. What is the solution?

Inform

God's great desire is for "all men to be saved and to come to a knowledge of the truth" (1 Timothy 2:4). To that end, He sent apostles and prophets to share His message of Law and Gospel. Through them, He called people to repentance and to saving faith in His Son. The message was revealed in its entirety when God sent the incarnate Word, Jesus Christ, into the world. Read the following lesson summaries.

Jeremiah 26:8–15—God sent Jeremiah to preach a message of repentance to the city of Jerusalem. Jeremiah did as God commanded Him. However, priests, prophets, and people rejected God's Word and sought to kill Jeremiah. Comfortable with their self-righteousness, they wanted a "feel-good" message instead. They put Jeremiah on trial. Unflinchingly, he repeated the message that God had given him to proclaim. He concluded by reminding them that the message was not his. It was, in fact, from God.

Philippians 3:17–4:1—Paul begins by urging the Philippians to imitate him. The example that Paul set before them was of a life lived in service to God. Paul knew there were other examples that the Philippians might be tempted to follow. The people around them were concerned with earthly desires. Paul told the Philippians not to hold onto those earthly things because Christian citizenship is in heaven. Paul encouraged them (and us!) to stand firm in the Lord.

Luke 13:31–35—The Pharisees sought to discourage Jesus by saying that if He went to Jerusalem, Herod would arrest Him. After all, Herod had John the Baptist arrested because of the uncomfortable message he preached. How much more uncomfortable Herod would be with the message of Jesus! Jesus, however, knew that God's clock was ticking toward the completion of His plan for the salvation of sinful and rebellious people. Thus Jesus would continue on, with His sights set on Jerusalem and the events that would take place during Holy Week. What compelled Him was His love for these rebellious people who, time and again, stoned and killed His messengers. His desire was that they would acclaim Him as "He who comes in the name of the Lord."

1. In Jeremiah's rebuke to the people of Jerusalem, why did his reference to "Shiloh" anger them so? Read Jeremiah 26:6; 1 Samuel 4:1–10; and Psalm 78:56–64.

2. Did God want to destroy Jerusalem? What was His purpose in sending Jeremiah to speak His message of warning? Do you know of other cities that were given warnings similar to this one? Read about the city of Ninevah in Jonah 3:1–10. Would you have expected the same reaction from the residents of Jerusalem? Why or why not?

3. What was the "feel-good" message the people of Jerusalem wanted to hear? Read Jeremiah 28:1–4. Who was God's messenger—Jeremiah or Hananiah? How do we know? How did the people of Jerusalem know? Read Jeremiah 28:15–17.

4. Paul encouraged people to imitate him. Read 1 Corinthians 4:16; 11:1. Ultimately, who was he encouraging people to imitate through his example? Read Ephesians 5:1.

5. Because of sin, individuals, societies, and civilizations will live as enemies of the cross. Paul mentions this briefly in Philippians 3:18–19 and in greater detail in Romans 1:18–32. According to Philippians 3:20–21, where do we get the power to live as God's people? Read also Ephesians 1:19–22.

6. The Gospel lesson gives us a picture of Christ's determined love. What specific things does Jesus say that indicate His determination?

7. What Holy Week events are foreshadowed by Christ? On whose word and work will these events focus? How does that make Jesus different from Jeremiah or Paul?

Connect

"Don't shoot the messenger." The bearer of unpopular news always risks having the anger of his audience vented at him. Such was certainly the case with Jeremiah. St. Paul's life was often at risk, and he died a martyr's death. And then there was Jesus. He was not only the messenger, He was also the message (John 1:14).

From the days of the great persecutions under the Roman emperors to today, many live as "enemies of the cross" (Philippians 3:18). One famous historian has suggested that more Christians have been martyred in the twentieth century than in all previous centuries put together. The word "martyr" means "to witness." In other words, martyrs seal their witness with their own deaths.

1. Should we expect people to still reject those whom God sends to speak the message of Law and Gospel? Read Colossians 1:21.

2. Why is the message of sin and grace an unpopular message for many people?

3. Not all people respond to the Law and Gospel with anger and hatred. Some respond with faith and love. How are the barriers of unbelief broken down? Read 1 Corinthians 12:2–3.

4. In your sharing of the message of sin and grace with others, what kind of responses did you expect? What kind of responses did you receive?

5. Is it worth all the hassle? How would St. Paul have responded to that question?

6. How does the certainty that we will go to heaven comfort us?

Vision

During This Week

1. Pray for your pastor as he brings God's Word to your congregation "in season and out of season" (2 Timothy 4:2).

2. Pray for opportunities to speak the Good News of Jesus Christ to those around you. Especially pray for the people with whom you will share the message, so that they will receive the message with faith and joy.

3. Make a point to speak a word of thanks and appreciation to those who have been God's messengers to you over the years.

Closing Worship

Sing or speak together "I'm But a Stranger Here" (*LW* 515).
> I'm but a stranger here, heav'n is my home;
> Earth is a desert drear, heav'n is my home.
> Danger and sorrow stand round me at every hand;
> Heav'n is my fatherland, heav'n is my home.
>
> What though the tempest rage, heav'n is my home;
> Short is my pilgrimage, heav'n is my home;
> And time's wild wintry blast soon shall be overpast;
> I shall reach home at last, heav'n is my home.
>
> Therefore I murmur not, heav'n is my home;
> Whate'er my earthly lot, heav'n is my home;
> And I shall surely stand there at my Lord's right hand.
> Heav'n is my fatherland, heav'n is my home.

Scripture Lessons for Next Sunday

In preparation for the Third Sunday in Lent, read Exodus 3:1–8a, 10–15; 1 Corinthians 10:1–13; and Luke 13:1–9.

Session 3

The Third Sunday in Lent

(Exodus 3:1–8a, 10–15; 1 Corinthians 10:1–13;
Luke 13:1–9)

Focus

Theme: A Word about Clubhouse Christianity

Law/Gospel Focus

At times, because of sin, Christians can become complacent about their faith. Through His Son, God forgives these sins and all others, calling us to live lives that reflect saving faith.

Objectives

That by the power of the Holy Spirit at work in our hearts through His Word, we will
1. repent of the shallowness that we so often exhibit in our relationship with God;
2. grow in a deeper appreciation of the life of faith to which God has called us and in our understanding of what it means to live as children of our heavenly Father;
3. recognize the gifts that God has given to all Christians to enable and empower us to live lives worthy of our calling;
4. commit ourselves to more frequent attendance at the Lord's Supper, to more regular attention to God's Word in worship and private devotion, and to regular and ongoing study of God's Word for personal growth and strength.

Opening Worship

Read responsively Psalm 90:1–12.

Leader: Lord, You have been our dwelling place throughout all generations.

Participants: Before the mountains were born or You brought forth the earth and the world, from everlasting to everlasting You are God.

Leader: You turn men back to dust, saying, "Return to dust, O sons of men."

Participants: For a thousand years in Your sight are like a day that has just gone by, or like a watch in the night.

Leader: You sweep men away in the sleep of death; they are like the new grass of the morning—though in the morning it springs up new, by evening it is dry and withered.

Participants: We are consumed by Your anger and terrified by Your indignation.

Leader: You have set our iniquities before You, our secret sins in the light of Your presence.

Participants: All our days pass away under Your wrath; we finish our years with a moan.

Leader: The length of our days is 70 years—or 80, if we have the strength; yet their span is but trouble and sorrow, for they quickly pass, and we fly away.

Participants: Who knows the power of Your anger? For Your wrath is as great as the fear that is due You. Teach us to number our days aright, that we may gain a heart of wisdom.

Introduction

"Membership has its privileges."

That well-marketed advertising cliche unfortunately could be used to describe the attitude that many have toward their faith, their relationship with God, and their relationship with the church. Pastors can tell of people they have never met before showing up and demanding to have their baby baptized ("done" is the word that is often used) or a marriage solemnized.

Some inactive members need the caring ministry of the local congregation to draw them back into the active fellowship of the church. Others have a "clubhouse" mentality about their church. They've been baptized and confirmed. That, in essence, is their "membership card." And as long as things are going well in their lives, they have no time or need to worship their Lord or to offer their lives in service to Him.

What is worse is that, although they possess their "membership cards," it's impossible to tell from their words or actions that they are Christians.

A man was invited to go hunting over the weekend with some associates at work. He expressed concern to his wife over the fact that these people didn't really hunt. They would use the weekend as an excuse to get drunk, tell filthy stories, and engage in other disgusting behavior. The man decided to go anyway. On returning from the "hunting" trip, his wife asked how it went. "Great," he said. "They never even found out that I am a Christian!"

1. The involvement of "clubhouse Christians" in the church is often described by the phrase "hatched, matched, and dispatched." In other words, church is important to them only for Baptisms, marriages, and funerals. Are these events part of their faith or part of their culture? What is the danger in this kind of attitude?

2. It would be easy to become self-righteous about this issue. Don't forget that the Pharisees, whom Jesus often chastised for their "clubhouse" mentality, were very religious people who regularly went to the temple. One can just as easily take on a hypocritical outward appearance of godliness. How does this happen?

3. On what basis has God called us to a life of faith? In your own words, describe that life of faith. How have you lived up to it?

Inform

Read the lessons appointed for today. Then read the lesson summaries.

Exodus 3:1–8a, 10–15—Moses, raised in the court of the Egyptian pharaoh, was forced to flee after he killed an Egyptian who had beaten a Hebrew slave. Moses left Egypt and spent many years tending the flock of his father-in-law. As Moses was tending a flock near Mount Horeb, the angel of the Lord appeared to him in the flames of a burning bush. God revealed Himself to Moses as the God of Abraham, Isaac, and Jacob—the great I AM. He called Moses to lead the Israelites out of slavery in Egypt by the power and authority of His great name.

1 Corinthians 10:1–13—St. Paul briefly recounts how God delivered the Israelites as He had promised Moses. Sadly, in spite of the great things God had done to deliver His people, many continued to live in spiritual slavery to sin. They rejected the covenant relationship that God had so graciously provided. The rebellious Israelites, in choosing to live outside of that relationship, by default chose God's wrath and anger, which He poured out upon them. Christians share in the same wondrous grace as the ancient Israelites. On the one hand, we are warned to be careful lest we fall. On the other hand, God will always be faithful to us and gives us the comforting promise that He will provide everything we need to stay faithful to Him in the time of temptation.

Luke 13:1–9—The Pharisees thought that if disaster befell them they were being directly punished by God and that if they did not suffer any tragedies in their lives God was pleased with them. Jesus set the record straight. He reminded the Pharisees that Pilate had killed Galileans while they made a religious sacrifice. Eighteen people had died when the tower in Siloam fell on them. They were no more guilty than anyone else in Jerusalem. Jesus told the Pharisees that they and all of Israel needed to repent. The parable of the fig tree points out the need and urgency for them to repent.

1. Read Exodus 2:23–25 and 3:7. Describe the condition of the Israelites. What were they able to contribute to their own deliverance? On what basis did God show concern for the Israelites?

2. What was to be the response of the Israelites to this great deliverance? Read 3:12, 15.

3. To what other deliverance events does St. Paul refer in the Epistle lesson? How did God provide for His people?

4. What was the response of some of the Israelites? Read 1 Corinthians 10:7–10. How did God react?

5. What unique temptations did the Israelites face that we don't have to worry about? Are there any temptations that we face that the Israelites didn't need to worry about?

6. We will be tempted; there is no question of that. What does God do for us in times of temptation?

7. In the parable of the fig tree, what did the owner of the vineyard expect? Did he have a right to expect it? How might the fig tree be compared to "clubhouse Christians"? Did the owner have the right to cut down the tree? What did he do that reminds us of God's mercy?

Connect

A young athlete purchased a membership at a local fitness club. As time passed, he worked out at the club less and less. He never neglected to tell his friends, however, that he did indeed belong to a fitness club. In time, he stopped going altogether, although he still paid the annual membership fee. He felt it was important to keep up appearances with his business associates. He continued to carry his membership card with him and always told his friends about his membership in the club. His growing paunch, however, told a different story. The day of reckoning came when, at age 40 and 100 pounds overweight, he suffered his first heart attack. In the emergency room at the hospital he said to the medical team that was attending him, "I just don't understand it. I have a membership in an exclusive fitness club."

1. Membership in a congregation is important. Read Hebrews 10:25. What does your congregation offer to you to help strengthen your faith? Why is it important to receive this help?

2. How does your congregation help you live out your Christian faith at work, at school, or at home?

3. What particular gifts has God given to you to share with others in your life of Christian service?

4. Because of His great love for each of us, God gives us gifts of grace, mercy, and peace whenever we gather to hear the Gospel preached. How do these gifts help in times of trial or temptation?

Vision

During This Week

1. Many of us fall into the habit of being nourished in our faith on Sundays and neglecting to exercise our faith during the week. Take some time every day for personal Bible study and prayer.

2. Find your baptismal certificate. Using a concordance, look up passages in the Bible that have to do with Baptism. Begin to draw on your baptismal blessings for spiritual strength as you face the challenges of each day.

3. Look for ways in which you can help people find their way back into an active, productive Christian life.

Closing Worship

End your time of study together by sharing one prayer request per person. Ask for volunteers to pray for that need or request.

Scripture Lessons for Next Sunday

In preparation for the Fourth Sunday in Lent, read Isaiah 12:1–6; 1 Corinthians 1:18–31; and Luke 15:1–3, 11–32.

Session 4

The Fourth Sunday in Lent

(Isaiah 12:1–6; 1 Corinthians 1:18–31; Luke 15:1–3, 11–32)

Focus

Theme: The Foolishness of God Overcomes the Folly of People

Law/Gospel Focus

We foolishly turn away from God when we deny His Word and His ownership of us and embrace fame, fortune, and fun as life's ultimate goals. But when life becomes intolerable and God's Law works in our hearts to make us see the folly of our godless ways, God Himself, in Christ Jesus, reclaims us and saves us by means of the Gospel.

Objectives

Through the reading and study of God's Word today, we pray that the Holy Spirit will

1. enable us to understand the real foolishness of isolating ourselves from God by living a life contrary to His Word and separate from His love and presence;
2. lead us to know the reality of God's undying love for us in Christ Jesus;
3. cause us to repent of and cease any activities that would draw us away from God and His Word;
4. aid us in knowing, accepting, and embracing the "foolishness" of the Gospel of Jesus Christ as God's wisdom for our salvation;
5. enable and empower us to change those aspects of our lifestyles that currently hinder us from living out our faith in Jesus Christ.

Introduction

It took some courage, but Johanna picked up the phone and called her pastor. "Pastor," she said with a quivering voice, "Mom's done it again! She's left Bradley and has moved in with a man who was once her neighbor. I don't know what to do!" The pastor felt Johanna's pain but also felt sick in the pit of his stomach because he knew that Johanna's mother was in trouble again. This was the third time that Shawna had done this kind of thing. She had now been unfaithful to her third husband. What Johanna did not know was that her mother had been in to see the pastor only three weeks earlier, after Bradley had announced that he did not love her and never had.

The pastor calmed Johanna and then began trying to reach Shawna, which was no easy task since she had moved into a mobile home on acreage 15 miles away. After several attempts, however, the pastor was able to reach Shawna and arrange a meeting. Shawna shuffled dejectedly into his office. She could hardly look the pastor in the eye because she knew in her heart that what she had done was against God's will. She explained that with Bradley gone and this man willing to "love" her, she felt she had to do what she did. The pastor, with great love and grace-filled words, explained to her that he cared about her and her daughter and was worried for her and Johanna's safety, both physical and spiritual. The pastor carefully shared God's Word regarding sexual activity outside of marriage and the breaking of the marriage vow. He explained that no good could come of this relationship. That meeting ended with the pastor telling her that although he cared deeply for her, as long as she remained in this situation he could not give her the Lord's Supper.

A few months passed, during which time Shawna continued to attend church. Then one day Shawna and Bradley showed up at church together. She asked for another meeting with the pastor. Shawna had taken her pastor's advice and had continued reading the Bible and worshiping. Although it had taken a little time, the Word of God had done its work in her heart. Shawna smiled at her pastor and said, "Pastor, I knew that things were not right when I was with Ed, and I felt guilty all the time. One day I was looking for some place to begin reading in the Bible and I ended up reading the entire Book of Hosea. Pastor, I realize that I have been Gomer, the unfaithful wife, and reading that book prompted me to call Bradley and ask to meet with him. He was as miserable as I was, and he was willing to talk about getting back together. We both recognize that we need help in putting our relationship back together. Bradley and I want to meet with you for counseling."

Shawna and Bradley did meet with the pastor, confessed their sins before God and each other, and received God's absolution. The same Word of God that brought Shawna to repentance enabled Bradley to forgive her and her to forgive Bradley for his actions that contributed to their breakup.

They are now, with God's help, in the process of putting their lives back together as husband and wife as they live in the full forgiveness of Christ. The true love generated by Christ's love for us is now the active ingredient in their relationship and in their home.

1. Have you ever witnessed a fellow Christian, maybe even someone very close to you, suddenly turn their back on God and begin living, knowingly and willingly, according to the flesh?

2. What was the result of their foolish living?

3. Have you witnessed God's Word coming into people's lives through someone close to them—maybe a pastor, a relative, or a close friend? What was the result?

Inform

Read the lessons appointed for this day. Then read the following summaries.

Isaiah 12:1–6—Isaiah proclaims God's revelation of who He is when he says, "God is my salvation." Then, in recognition of that truth, he responds, "I will trust and not be afraid." Isaiah, faithful in the ability of God to save him and the nation of Israel from all its foes, goes on to sing the praises of God, remembering that it is from God that one receives power and strength. Isaiah points ahead to a future time when all nations will join him in his praise of the one true God. He encourages his readers to sing to the Lord God and let the whole world know about the Gospel—the Good News that salvation belongs alone to God and to all who believe and trust in Him and His promises. And then, finally, he exhorts the people of Israel, his own people, those who hold the promise of a Savior, to sing and shout because God truly lives among them.

1 Corinthians 1:18–31—St. Paul maintains that the message of the cross (that is, the Gospel of Jesus Christ) is "foolishness" to the unbeliever ("those who are perishing"). But, he says, it is "the power of God" for believers. He assures us that although the wise of the world will reject the message of the cross, we who are saved by faith in Jesus according to the grace of God need to remember that God's "foolishness" (the cross and His plan of salvation via the cross) is wiser than all of mankind's wisdom put together. This message is also a "stumbling block" to the Jews, who should have

believed but turned their hearts to their own man-made religion.

Luke 15:1–3, 11–32—In this section of Scripture, Jesus tells the parable of the prodigal son or the loving father, depending on your point of view. In this parable, a young man who wants to experience all the fun and pleasures of the world requests his inheritance from his father. The father agrees to the request and the son leaves the father's household. In a faraway land he squanders all of his money and ends up working for a farmer, taking care of pigs. He is so desperate that he eats the pods that the pigs are eating. Finally, he comes to his senses and returns to his father's farm, hoping that at least he might get a job there as one of his father's servants. To his great surprise, his father runs to greet him, calls for a big celebration, and restores him to his former position as son. The older son, who had remained at the farm, is incensed that his father should so welcome and restore his younger brother's fortunes, but the father ends the parable by saying, "My son, you are always with me, and everything I have is yours. But we had to celebrate and be glad, because this brother of yours was dead and is alive again; he was lost and now is found."

1. What important characteristic of God is revealed in all three readings?

2. What is the point that God makes in 1 Corinthians 1:18–31 regarding what is really foolish? What does the world see as foolish? What is foolish in God's eyes?

3. Describe the foolishness of the son in Jesus' parable (Luke 15:11–32).

4. How might the reaction of the father be considered foolish in the eyes of the world?

5. It has been said that "grace" is the unmerited love of God in Christ Jesus. Another definition is *God's Riches At Christ's Expense*. Describe how God demonstrated grace in each of the readings.

Connect

1. Share some examples of people whom you have known who refuse to believe the Gospel. What are some excuses they use?

2. In the parable of the prodigal son we see the folly of youth depicted—how we often run away from God, demanding for ourselves all of His blessings but wanting to live our lives outside of His will. What kind of lifestyles can we observe today that might correspond to the prodigal son's lifestyle?

3. How should the church minister to modern-day "prodigals"? What is the message that they need to hear from God's people today?

4. Do unbelievers today still view the cross of Jesus Christ as "foolish"? What makes the cross so offensive to them?

5. How do Christians sometimes live as those without hope?

6. What is God's view of those who fall from the faith, involve themselves in lifestyles that are contrary to the Word of God, and separate themselves from God and the church?

Vision

During This Week

1. This week pray for one person or family with whom you are acquainted who has fallen away from the church and perhaps from the faith. Ask God to touch them with His Law, in order to help them see the foolishness of their rebellion against Him, and then with the Gospel, in order for them to experience the power of His grace and forgiveness.

2. As a family discuss together what might cause any member of your family to become inactive in the church and how to prevent that from happening.

Closing Worship

Read responsively by half verse the Introit for the Fourth Sunday in Lent.

Leader: Wait for the Lord;

Class: Be strong and take heart and wait for the Lord.

Leader: One thing I ask of the Lord, this is what I seek:
That I may dwell in the house of the Lord all the days of my life,
Class: To gaze upon the beauty of the Lord and to seek Him in His temple.
Leader: For in the day of trouble He will keep me safe in His dwelling;
Class: He will hide me in the shelter of His tabernacle and set me high upon a rock.
Leader: At His tabernacle will I sacrifice with shouts of joy;
Class: I will sing and make music to the Lord.
All: Glory be to the Father, and to the Son, and to the Holy Spirit; as it was in the beginning, is now, and will be forever. Amen.
Leader: Wait for the Lord;
Class: Be strong and take heart and wait for the Lord.

Scripture Lessons for Next Sunday

Read Isaiah 43:16–21; Philippians 3:8–12; and Luke 20:9–19 in preparation for the next session.

Session 5

The Fifth Sunday in Lent

(Isaiah 43:16–21; Philippians 3:8–12; Luke 20:9–19)

Focus

Theme: God Makes Us New in Christ

Law/Gospel Focus

People often choose to focus their lives on the accumulation of earthly wisdom, treasures, and philosophies. In His grace and mercy God never gives up trying to bring us into a saving relationship with Him through faith in Christ Jesus to save us for all eternity.

Objectives

Through the study of God's Word today, we pray that the Holy Spirit will
1. teach us how to recognize a life path that is dangerous to our spiritual health;
2. open our eyes to see that God is constantly calling us to forsake the influence of the world, the devil, and our own sinful desires, and to trust in Him alone both for our salvation and for direction in our life;
3. enable us to confess with St. Paul, "I consider everything a loss compared to the surpassing greatness of knowing Christ Jesus my Lord, for whose sake I have lost all things";
4. strengthen our faith as we recommit our lives to loving and serving the God who first loved and served us in Christ.

Opening Worship

Pray together:
Gracious Heavenly Father, we give You thanks and praise this day for revealing Your deep and abiding love for us in

the person and work of our Savior, Jesus Christ. Having created us and placed us upon the earth, You have given us the responsibility of caring for it as tenants responsible to You. By the power of Your Holy Spirit, give us the will and ability to care for Your creation. Through the study and reading of Your Word today, strengthen our faith, hope, and trust in You and our resolve to never allow anything worldly to get in the way of our faith and devotion to You. This we ask in Jesus' name. Amen.

Introduction

Tyrell had decided that the most important thing in his young life was basketball. After all, he wasn't a particularly great student, but a major university had offered him a full scholarship to play for them. And Tyrell really loved the game. Maybe that's why he excelled at it. He had been the top scorer and top rebounder during his high school years. He was now completing his first year at the university, and even though he was only a freshman, he had played first string and his team had made it all the way to the Final Four! His dedication and hard work were paying off, but Tyrell also realized that God was behind his success.

When he was only 12 years old, Tyrell had lost his father, and he saw then how God had blessed his mother and three older sisters with added strength. By pooling resources, his family had made sure that he had the best shoes and attended the best basketball camps. Tyrell knew that God had blessed him with a natural ability for the game. God had also given him a strong faith in Jesus as his Savior. Deep inside him was a stirring that made him think that maybe he should even consider becoming a pastor one day. But right now basketball was the most important thing in his life, and his athletic skills could possibly lead him to a lucrative NBA career someday.

Even though he was on the road many weekends during basketball season, Tyrell always tried to get to church on Sunday if he could. There his spirit was recharged as he heard the Good News of God's love for him in Christ Jesus. He was refreshed with Jesus' body and blood in Holy Communion. Even when he couldn't go to church, he and a couple of other teammates would study the Bible in their motel room and pray together.

That freshman year was great for Tyrell, and he felt proud to be a part of a team that had made it all the way to the Final Four. Ahead were three more years of studies and basketball. His skills increased, and with them came many individual trophies. Several NBA scouts were watching Tyrell, and in his senior year he was offered a shot at playing for one of the great NBA teams. He had a tough decision to make. That small voice, together with his pastor and his family, had on more than one occasion asked him to consider the holy ministry. On the other hand, an NBA career offered riches and influence and adoration by thousands. Which would he choose?

1. What advice would you give Tyrell? Why?

2. How important is the influence of family as young people look to the future and consider different vocations? Consider the importance of a family's faith relationship. Look at 2 Timothy 1:5–7 as you consider your answers.

3. Have you ever had a similar type of decision to make in your life? If so, share with the class how you reached your decision and especially how God helped you.

Tyrell, with the support of his family and his congregation, decided to become a pastor and enrolled in a seminary the year after his senior year at the university. He now serves his Lord in a parish and has never regretted his decision to enter the pastoral ministry.

Inform

Read the appointed lessons. Then read the lesson summaries.

Isaiah 43:16–21—This section of Isaiah's prophecy begins with a reminder to God's people of His saving action for them when He rescued them from the land of Egypt by His own miraculous power. Not only did He draw the forces of Pharoah out of Egypt into the Red Sea, but He snuffed them out like a wick. As great a saving action as that was for Israel, God tells them that He is about to do something entirely new. He explains that He is making a way in the desert and streams in the wasteland and will bless His people, Israel, whom He chose and formed, so that they will believe in Him and proclaim His praise.

Philippians 3:8–14—St. Paul says that he considers everything earthly to be a loss compared to the supreme value of knowing Jesus Christ as his Savior. He considers everything else useless in comparison to Christ, and so he declares that he has willingly lost everything. God has endowed him and all Christians with a righteousness that is not of their own making but comes simply through faith in Jesus Christ. Paul's main aim in life is to know Christ and the power of His resurrection. Paul is willing to share in Jesus' sufferings and become like Him in his death. He ends by saying that he is pressing on toward that eternal life for which Christ had taken hold of him on the road to Damascus.

Luke 20:9–19—Jesus tells the parable of the tenants. The parable relates the story of a landowner going on a trip and renting his land to some tenant farmers. At harvest time he sends representatives to collect his portion of the crop (the rent), but the farmers are greedy and beat his representatives, refusing to pay their rent. Then the landowner sends his own son to collect the rent, but the tenants kill him. As a result, Jesus says that the landowner will give the land to other tenants after first killing those responsible for the death of his son. The people who were listening to Jesus were horrified and said, "May this never be!" They recognized that this parable was spoken against them. As a result, the teachers of the law and the chief priests began looking for a way to arrest Jesus.

1. How did God save Israel from slavery in the land of Egypt and keep His promise to Abraham made centuries before (Genesis 12)?

2. What was the "new thing" that God planned for His people? See Isaiah 7:14.

3. How did Paul describe the "new thing" that God had done? How important was it for Paul that God had accomplished this?

4. What gift did God give to Paul that He also gives to all who believe, making us acceptable to Him?

5. What evil did Jesus expose in the parable of the tenants that accused the teachers of the law and the chief priests?

6. Who specifically are the "tenants" in Jesus' parable? Why are they condemned?

Connect

1. Some churches have publicly declared that there are many different ways to eternal life and that Christians who confess that salvation is possible only through faith in Christ alone are wrong. How would you respond? See Ephesians 2:8–10 and Romans 3:21–26; 5:1.

2. Who today would be the "tenant farmers" in Jesus' parable? Check out John 14:5–7 as you answer.

3. How do you manage God's physical gifts (your money, time, etc.) so that you show that God and His will for you in Christ Jesus are most important in your life?

4. Are there times in your life when the lure of the world and its riches entice you to stop putting Jesus first? If so, share how that happens.

5. Can you say with St. Paul that you would consider everything physical in this world "garbage" in comparison with knowing Jesus Christ as your Savior? Read Romans 8:38–39.

Vision

During This Week

1. Do a family inventory this week to see how much of your time, energy, and money you actually use in service to the Lord. If changes are in order, then pray that the Holy Spirit will strengthen you and lead you to more dedicated service to Christ and your neighbor.

2. Visit a nursing home near you and seek someone there to visit to whom you can bring the love of Jesus through that visit, a hug, or maybe even a small gift.

Closing Worship

Pray Psalm 121 responsively.

Leader: I lift up my eyes to the hills—
Class: Where does my help come from?
Leader: My help comes from the LORD,
Class: The maker of heaven and earth.
Leader: He will not let your foot slip—
Class: He who watches over you will not slumber;
Leader: Indeed He who watches over Israel
Class: Will neither slumber nor sleep.
Leader: The LORD watches over you—
Class: The LORD is your shade at your right hand;
Leader: The sun will not harm you by day,
Class: Nor the moon by night.
Leader: The LORD will keep you from all harm—
Class: He will watch over your life;
Leader: The LORD will watch over your coming and going
Class: Both now and forevermore.

Scripture Lessons for Next Sunday

Read Deuteronomy 32:36–39; Philippians 2:5–11; and Luke 22:1–23 in preparation for the next session.

The Sixth Sunday in Lent

(Deuteronomy 32:36–39; Philippians 2:5–11;
Luke 22:1–23)

Focus

Theme: Jesus Emptied Himself So That We Might Be Saved

Law/Gospel Focus

By nature we are born sinful and guilty of committing many evil deeds in the eyes of God as we fail to live up to His commandments. But in His great love and mercy God sent us His only begotten Son, Jesus Christ, who emptied Himself, becoming a human being like us so that He could take our place under the Law and then die on the cross and rise again to save us from the damning consequences of our sin.

Objectives

Through the study of God's Word today, we pray that the Holy Spirit will

1. enable us to see the depth of our own depravity as sinful human beings who deserve only God's condemnation because of our failure to live perfectly as His people;
2. reveal clearly God's eternal love and mercy in sending Christ Jesus to a terrible death on a cross for our sakes so that He might pay the penalty for our sins;
3. help us to realize that having been saved by God's grace in Christ, we are now forgiven and free to empty ourselves as we give thanks to God and serve our neighbor;
4. give us the ability to apply the great truths of these lessons to our everyday lives and to live in joy and freedom as those who have been redeemed, restored, and forgiven by God, through Jesus Christ our Lord and Savior;

5. enable us to appreciate Jesus' special gift to us—His true body and blood in the Sacrament of Holy Communion—which forgives our sins and strengthens our faith.

Opening Worship

Leader: As we begin our lesson today we remember the Upper Room where our Lord and Savior, Jesus Christ, gathered His disciples for the celebration of the Passover. There He instituted His own special supper for the strengthening of our faith.

Our Lord Jesus Christ, on the same night on which He was betrayed, took bread, and when He had given thanks, He broke it and gave it to the disciples and said, "Take, eat; this is My body, which is given for you. This do in remembrance of Me." In the same way He also took the cup after supper, and when He had given thanks, He gave it to them, saying, "Drink of it, all of you; this is My blood of the new covenant, which is shed for you for the forgiveness of sins. This do, as often as you drink it, in remembrance of Me."

Sing together "Draw Near and Take the Body of the Lord" (*LW* 240).

> Draw near and take the body of the Lord,
> And drink the holy blood for you outpoured;
> Offered was He for greatest and for least,
> Himself the victim and Himself the priest.
>
> He who His saints in this world rules and shields,
> To all believers life eternal yields;
> With heav'nly bread He makes the hungry whole,
> Gives living waters to the thirsting soul.
>
> Come forward then with faithful hearts sincere,
> And take the pledges of salvation here.
> O Lord, our hearts with grateful thanks endow
> As in this feast of love You bless us now.

Introduction

There was once a pastor who had served in a district office for 10 years. At age 49 he received a call from a parish in the very town where he had lived and worshiped for many years. It was the same parish that he had been assigned to right out of the seminary some 25 years earlier. As unusual as the circumstances were, he felt compelled to accept the call and was installed as pastor of the congregation a few weeks later.

He was excited to be back in the parish ministry once again, but was also somewhat apprehensive as he realized that he had been "out of the saddle," so to speak, for some 10 years. Returning to the parish he had served as a young man in the ministry would be somewhat of a challenge. Would he be able to serve effectively as a parish pastor once again? Would the people accept his pastoral leadership? Would he be able to counsel and bring the Gospel effectively to those in the hospital and nursing homes? These questions and others plagued him as he prepared to move into his new office at the church.

The first Sunday after his installation he had led the people in the Service of the Word, spoken the words of institution for the Lord's Supper, and was about to begin serving his people the true body and blood of Jesus, when he suddenly realized an important truth. As he looked into the faces of his parishioners kneeling in reverence before the Lord's altar, he saw shining through them real faith—simple, childlike faith—and it moved him deeply. Filled with emotion, he spoke the words, "Take and drink, this is the true blood of our Lord and Savior, Jesus Christ, shed FOR YOU on the cross of Calvary ... shed for the forgiveness of all our sins." It was at this point that God removed all of his concerns about being able to minister to these people. He realized that this was God's ministry, not his, and that God would work through him despite his weaknesses and failures, despite his fears. And then with joy the pastor dismissed those at the altar rail with the words, "Now, may this, the true body and blood of Jesus, strengthen and preserve you in the true faith, unto life everlasting. Depart in the peace and joy of sins forgiven for Jesus' sake."

And, as that group of people left the altar area, forgiven, refreshed, and cleansed of all sin, the pastor said a silent prayer of thanks to God for His special gifts and for fulfilling once again Jesus' promise: "Lo, I am with you always ..." The pastor's fear for his future ministry dissipated when he remembered the promises of God and realized God's presence and power in his life and in the life of His people through His Word and Sacraments.

1. From where does the power and ability to minister effectively come? See 2 Timothy 2:1 and Psalm 28:7–8.

2. What kind of spiritual power does God place into the Lord's Supper for all Christians? See Matthew 26:28 and 1 John 1:7.

3. What was this pastor's problem originally? In other words, why was he afraid as he moved back into parish ministry? In whom was he trusting when he feared the future?

4. Have you ever had a similar experience where you had to make an important decision in life and were apprehensive after having made it? If you asked the Lord for His guidance and direction through prayer, did He give it?

5. God, through His Sacraments, comes to us with power to forgive, renew, and strengthen us. How does this happen in Holy Baptism? In the Lord's Supper? See Titus 3:5–7; Matthew 26:28; Romans 6:8–9; 1 Peter 2:24; and Galatians 3:26–27.

Inform

Read the lessons appointed for the Sixth Sunday in Lent. Then read the lesson summaries.

Deuteronomy 32:36–39—Moses writes that God is both a God of judgment and a God of compassion. God asks those who have turned to the pagan gods where their gods are now that they are in trouble. He reiterates the truth that there is no other God than Himself and that the false gods of the pagans are no gods at all. These gods are helpless to do anything for the people. That is why God's people find only trouble when they put their trust in them. God declares to His people that He is the only true God—the author of life and death—a sovereign God out of whose hand no one can be snatched. Implicit in the reading is God's call to believe, trust, and worship Him alone.

Philippians 2:5–11—St. Paul says that our mindset should be the same as that of Christ Jesus, who did not hold on to His power, honor, and glory as the only begotten Son of God, but emptied Himself. He left heaven and the place of honor at the right hand of God the Father, came to earth as a human being, and then placed Himself under the sentence of death, even death on a cross. As a result, says St. Paul, God the Father exalted Him to the highest place and returned Him to heaven and His place of honor at His own right hand. All this happened so that every person on earth might confess Jesus as their Savior, worship Him, and proclaim this truth to the world so that God might be glorified.

Luke 22:1–23—In this reading we are told that Judas agrees to betray Jesus to the chief priests and the teachers of the law. Then the scene moves to the preparations for the celebration of the Passover by Jesus and His disciples. Jesus tells Peter and John to make the preparations, saying that they will meet a man carrying a jar of water and that they are to follow him to the house that he enters. There they will celebrate the Passover together. At this time Jesus does something rather remarkable. He changes the rubrics of the Passover meal and institutes the Sacrament of Holy Communion. Then He ends with a warning to the man who would betray Him.

1. If God is the author of life and death, why is it important for us to abandon the philosophies and religions of the world and concentrate on the Christian Gospel alone? See Matthew 7:14–15; John 3:36; 15:1ff.; and 1 John 2:24–25.

2. Describe what St. Paul means when he says that Jesus "emptied" Himself. Of what did He empty Himself?

3. Why did Jesus empty Himself and become an obedient servant? See 2 Corinthians 8:9.

4. As Jesus initiated the Lord's Supper for the first time with His disciples, He indicated that there was one among them who would betray Him. How do you think that this statement affected the disciples?

5. Jesus says that He will not eat the Passover or celebrate His new Supper again with His disciples until its fulfilment occurs in the kingdom of God. What do you think that He meant?

Connect

1. List some ways in which people today trust in false gods.

2. How do we get the message of Deuteronomy 32 across to people today? That is, how can we show that trusting in the true God both for forgiveness of sins and for physical blessings is the best course of action?

3. List as many ways as you can think of that God still blesses us today. List both physical and spiritual blessings that He grants us freely.

4. What does Jesus' emptying Himself mean for us?

5. How does the Epistle lesson indirectly motivate us to fulfill the Great Commission (Matthew 28:19)?

6. What comfort do you personally receive when you receive the Lord's Supper?

7. How might we empty ourselves in response to faith in Christ Jesus?

Vision

During This Week

1. Discuss with your family the real meaning of the Lord's Supper for you and its power to strengthen.

2. This week find a way to give yourself unselfishly to someone else. You might do something special for your mother or father or for a child in the family. You might choose to do something special for a person who cannot leave their home or a nursing facility.

Closing Worship

Pray together the following prayer:

Gracious God, heavenly Father, we thank and praise You for Your great love and mercy shown us in sending Jesus to die on the cross for us and then raising Him from the dead on that first Easter morning, victorious over sin, death, and the devil. Help us to live daily in the joy and freedom of knowing Jesus as our Savior and Friend. By the power of Your Holy Spirit, grant to us the gift of faithfulness to You and selfless service to those whom You have placed in our path through life. Grant us Your continual strengthening power that You offer freely in Your Word and Sacrament. In Jesus' name we pray. Amen.